Roald Dahl
The Storyteller

Jason Hook

HODDER
Wayland
an imprint of Hodder Children's Books

© 2003 White-Thomson Publishing Ltd

Produced by White-Thomson Publishing Ltd
2/3 St Andrew's Place, Lewes, BN7 1UP

Editor: Elaine Fuoco-Lang
Inside and Cover Design: Tim Mayer
Picture Research: Shelley Noronha –
   Glass Onion Pictures
Proofreader : Alison Cooper

Cover: Roald Dahl outside his writing shed.
Title page: Roald Dahl enjoyed writing horror and
suspense stories.

Published in Great Britain in 2003 by Hodder Wayland,
an imprint of Hodder Children's Books

This paperback edition published in 2004

British Library Cataloguing in Publication Data
Hook, Jason
   Roald Dahl. - (Famous Lives)
   1. Dahl, Roald, 1916 - Juvenile literature 2. Novelists,
   English - Biography - Juvenile literature
   I. Title
   823.9'14
ISBN 0 7502 4491 7

Printed in China

Hodder Children's Books
A division of Hodder Headline Limited
338 Euston Road, London, NW1 3BH

Acknowledgements: The publishers would like to thank
the Roald Dahl literary estate for their assistance with this
book.

Picture acknowledgements: Camera Press 4; Camera
Press/Richard Stonehouse 37, 45; Corbis 17, 23;
Ffotograph/Patricia Aithie 7; Hodder Wayland Picture
Library 18; Mary Evans 9, 10, 12; Pictorial Press 5, 29
© David Wolper, 25 © Guild/Disney/Allied filmmakers,
30, 35 © Portobello Productions, 41 © Warner/Lorimar,
43 © Columbia Tristar/Jersey; Popperfoto title page, 15,
19, 21, 22, 26, 32; Rex 24, 28, 32; Rex/LmcCombe/TPX
27; Roald Dahl literary estate cover, 6, 8, 11, 13, 14, 16,
34, 36, 40, 44; Topham 20, 31, 33, 38, 39.

Contents

The Inventing Room   4

My Father   6

Boy   8

The Chocolate Room   10

It's Off to Work We Go!   12

Going Solo   14

The Author   16

Adventure   18

Lamb to the Slaughter   20

Someone Like You   22

The Giant Peach   24

Family Life   26

The Chocolate Factory   28

November   30

The Second Miracle   32

The Champion of the World   34

My Father's Deep Dark Secret   36

Journey to a Dream Country   38

The Grand High Witch   40

The Third Miracle   42

The Magic Finger   44

Glossary   46

Further Information   46

Date Chart   47

Index   48

The Inventing Room

Hidden away in a garden shed, a giant of a man sits writing. His feet are propped against a battered suitcase, a blanket covers his legs, and on his lap rests the wooden board on which he works. A hole is cut in the back of his ancient armchair to stop it pressing against his aching spine.

'On the door it said, INVENTING ROOM – PRIVATE – KEEP OUT. Mr Wonka took a key from his pocket, leaned over the side of the boat, and put the key in the keyhole. "This is the most important room in the entire factory!" he said. "All my most secret new inventions are cooking and simmering in here!"'
Roald Dahl, *Charlie and the Chocolate Factory*, 1964.

Roald Dahl in the garden shed where he invented his characters.

Willy Wonka and the children, from the 1971 film Willy Wonka and the Chocolate Factory. *From left to right: Augustus Gloop, Violet Beauregarde, Charlie Bucket (standing in front of Willy Wonka), Veruca Salt and Mike Teevee.*

Scattered over a writing desk beside him is a collection of curious objects. Each offers a clue to the life he has led and the stories he has written. There is a heavy, silver ball, made entirely of chocolate wrappers; a carved grasshopper; his father's knife; a valve used in children's brain surgery; a model of a Hurricane fighter-plane; and a large bone, removed from his own hip.

These objects must weave a certain magic. For the writer is Roald Dahl, and it is in this hideaway that he invents his famous characters: James and the Giant Peach, Willy Wonka, Matilda, and the BFG.

My Father

Harald and Sofie Dahl, Roald's parents, on their wedding day.

Roald Dahl lived an unusual life, so it is perhaps not surprising that his story starts even before he was born! His father, Harald Dahl, believed that his son would grow up to love beautiful things if he experienced them from inside the womb. So, Harald insisted on taking his pregnant wife, Sofie, on 'glorious walks' through the beautiful countryside.

Harald was Norwegian, but had made his fortune as a shipbroker in Wales. He was a single-minded man, who had overcome terrible misfortune to achieve his success. When he was fourteen, his left arm had been

'When I was a boy, I was an avid collector of birds' eggs ... To open a drawer and see thirty different very beautiful eggs nestling in their compartments on pink cotton wool was a lovely sight.'
Roald Dahl, *My Year*, 1983.

The church in Cardiff Bay, Llandaff, where Roald Dahl was christened.

amputated after an accident. In 1907, his first wife had died leaving him with two children.

Harald had remarried after meeting Sofie Hesselberg on a trip home to Norway. With Sofie, Harald had four more children. Roald, their only boy, was born on 13 September 1916, in Llandaff, near Cardiff. The glorious walks seem to have worked – he would grow up to love collecting beautiful objects: from birds' eggs and roses, to antiques and paintings.

Boy

Both Roald and his father would suffer misfortune throughout their lives. When Roald was three, while his mother was pregnant again, his seven-year-old sister, Astri, died from appendicitis. Two months later, his grieving father died from pneumonia, or perhaps from a broken heart. Years later, the heroes of many of Roald Dahl's stories would be orphans or children with a single parent.

Dahl on holiday with his family in Norway.

When Roald was a young boy his mother told him folk-tales about Norwegian giants like the one illustrated here.

'My grandmother was Norwegian. The Norwegians know all about witches, for Norway, with its black forests and icy mountains, is where the first witches came from.'
Roald Dahl, *The Witches*, 1983.

But Roald's childhood was far from unhappy. Left a widow in a foreign country, Sofie moved into a smaller house and raised six children. Roald adored his mother, and remembered: 'Her children radiated round her like planets round a sun.'

Every summer, Sofie took the whole family on holiday to Norway. These were magical journeys for Roald, who listened wide-eyed to folk-tales about witches and giants that he would never forget. He kept a secret diary of his childhood adventures. But even as a child he needed a hideaway in which to write — a treehouse at the top of a horse chestnut tree.

The Chocolate Room

A 1929 advertisement for Cadbury's chocolate.

At the age of nine, Roald was packed off to boarding school. He went first to St Peter's, just over the English border, and then to Repton, a public school near Derby. Tall for his age, he was outstanding at sports. He was also a keen photographer, who found a new hideaway in the school darkroom. But Roald showed little promise in English or his other lessons.

At Repton, teachers and older boys terrorized younger pupils with brutal canings and vicious bullying. Dahl never got over this, and the theme of taking revenge on bullies would play a part in many of his stories.

'And it wasn't simply an ordinary enormous chocolate factory, either. It was the largest and most famous in the whole world! It was WONKA'S FACTORY, owned by a man called Mr Willy Wonka, the greatest inventor and maker of chocolates that there has ever been.'
Roald Dahl, *Charlie and the Chocolate Factory*, 1964.

Repton also provided Roald with a happier theme – chocolate! Cadbury's (the famous British chocolate manufacturer) sent their latest inventions to the school, so that pupils could taste them and award them marks. So began Dahl's lifelong love of chocolate. He dreamt of becoming an inventor for Cadbury's. Instead, he would one day write a story about the greatest chocolate inventor of them all.

Roald's first boarding school, St Peter's.

It's Off to Work We Go!

In his last term at Repton, Roald secretly kept a motorcycle on which to roar around the countryside. He said: 'It gave me an amazing feeling of winged majesty and of independence.'

A desire for even greater independence prompted him to accept a job with the Shell Oil Company. At first he was stuck behind a desk in London, where he built the ball of chocolate wrappers that would one day be kept in his writing hut. But he longed to sail to 'distant and magic lands'.

A 1929 advertisement for the Shell Oil Company.

In 1938, 22-year-old Roald was sent on a three-year posting to Dar es Salaam on the eastern coast of Africa. Here, he found the adventures he craved. He learnt to speak Swahili; visited diamond mines; and rescued a servant from a deadly black mamba snake. He also sold his first article, telling the true story of a local cook's wife who was rescued unharmed from a lion's jaws.

'Oh, lion dear, could I not make
You happy with a lovely steak
Could I entice you from your lair
With rabbit pie or roasted hare?
The lion smiled and shook his head.
He came up very close and said,
"The meat I am about to chew
Is neither steak nor chops.
IT'S YOU."'
Roald Dahl, 'The Lion' from *Dirty Beasts*, 1983.

Dahl, aged 22, in Dar es Salaam, where he had his first great adventures.

13

Going Solo

Dahl in Nairobi at the start of the Second World War wearing the flying gear he loved.

When the Second World War broke out in 1939, Roald seized the opportunity for even greater adventure. He drove his battered old car 1,000 kilometres to Nairobi, Kenya, and enlisted in the Royal Air Force (RAF).

'Oh, it was wonderful to be flying on the back of this great swan! It was wonderful to be up in the air and to feel the air swishing past his face.'
Roald Dahl, *The Minpins*, 1991.

Training to be a pilot was the happiest time of Dahl's life. He never forgot the joy of soaring gloriously through the air while watching the wild animals sweep beneath him, and many of his children's stories would include amazing flights. He was so tall that his head actually stuck up out of the cockpit, and the other pilots nicknamed him Lofty.

An RAF plane in Egypt during the Second World War.

On 19 September 1940, with his training complete, Roald was ordered to fly to an airfield in Egypt to join his squadron. Becoming lost, and running short of fuel, he crash-landed in the desert. His head lurched forward into the plane's gun-sight, driving his nose back into his skull. Blinded and bleeding, Roald somehow dragged himself clear. Moments later, his plane burst into flames.

The Author

Dahl in a tented camp in Greece in 1941.

'Hell's bells, what was that? Felt like she was hit somewhere. Blast this stick; it won't come back. They must have got my tail plane and jammed my elevators.'
Roald Dahl, *Shot Down in Libya*, 1942.

Despite spending six months in hospital to recover from his injuries, Dahl refused to be sent home. He finally joined up with his squadron in Greece, and successfully shot down at least five enemy planes in combat. But in the summer of 1941, severe headaches forced him to return to England.

A golden opportunity now came Dahl's way. Believing that this towering, talkative flying ace might help to attract American support in the war, the Air Ministry sent him across to Washington D.C. as a diplomat.

The British writer C. S. Forester, who was famous for writing stories about a naval officer called Horatio Hornblower.

In Washington Dahl had a fortunate meeting with a famous author called C. S. Forester who wanted to write about fighter pilots during the war and asked Dahl to provide some notes. Instead, Dahl wrote a complete story, a thrilling mix of fact and fiction. The *Saturday Evening Post* immediately published it under the title *Shot Down In Libya*. Dahl received a cheque for $900, and Forester asked him: 'Did you know you were a writer?' His new career had begun.

Adventure

The next part of Roald Dahl's life sounds like something from one of his stories. British Intelligence recruited him to spy on the most powerful people in Washington. Other writers were doing similar work, and Dahl was soon mixing with Noel Coward, Ernest Hemingway and Ian Fleming, the creator of James Bond.

Hollywood actress Ava Gardner with the writer Ernest Hemingway, whom Dahl met in Washington.

To meet the rich and famous, Dahl used his talents as a storyteller. He had continued to write short stories about the war, and he would recite these at dinner parties. One of his tales, *The Gremlins*, was his first children's story. It was based on a popular RAF myth about little imps causing mechanical problems on aircraft. It found its way on to the desk of Walt Disney, and, at the age of 25, Dahl was summoned to Hollywood.

> **'He saw a little man, scarcely more than six inches high, with a large round face and a little pair of horns growing out of his head. On his legs were a pair of shiny black suction boots, which made it possible for him to remain standing on the wing at 300 miles an hour.'**
> Roald Dahl, *The Gremlins*, 1943.

Although plans for a film were cancelled, Disney published the story. It became popular with the wife of President Franklin D. Roosevelt, and Dahl now found himself having dinner at the White House!

Five men had to operate the camera used to photograph cartoons in the Walt Disney Hollywood Studios in the 1940s.

Lamb to the Slaughter

When the war ended in 1945, Dahl returned to England to live with his mother in the rural village of Great Missenden, Buckinghamshire. Dahl enjoyed country life, and spent time with the local poachers. He still loved to collect beautiful things, and made a living by buying paintings and antiques for his new wealthy friends in the USA.

All the while, Dahl was writing. In 1946, a collection of his war stories, *Over to You*, was published to excellent reviews. He then wrote one of the first novels about nuclear war, *Sometime Never*, but this was poorly received.

Dahl had also started inventing strange, dark tales, with unexpected twists at the end. In *Lamb to the Slaughter*, a woman kills her husband with a frozen leg of lamb, then cooks the murder weapon and serves it to detectives. In *Skin*, a man sells a picture by a famous artist, even though it is tattooed on his back. Such sinister plots would bring Dahl the fame he craved.

Great Missenden, Buckinghamshire, where Dahl lived with his mother after the Second World War.

'It wasn't nasty. I thought it was hilarious. What's horrible is basically funny. In fiction.' Roald Dahl talking about *Lamb to the Slaughter*, 1954.

Dahl's fascination with horror would influence his adult and children's stories.

Someone Like You

At the age of 35, Dahl accepted a friend's invitation to move to New York. There, at exactly 6.45 p.m. on 20 October 1952, he found himself at a dinner party seated beside the famous Hollywood actress Patricia Neal. We know the time, because Dahl would later frame the page from his diary.

'I tried to join the conversation but he totally ignored me. I was infuriated and tried to pretend his rudeness did not bother me in the least, but by the end of the evening, I had made up my mind that I loathed Roald Dahl.'
Patricia Neal recalls her first meeting with Roald Dahl in her autobiography *As I Am*, 1988.

The bright lights of New York where Dahl met Patricia Neal in 1952. At first Patricia Neal disliked Dahl, but soon grew to love him.

**Dahl and his wife
Patricia Neal,
pictured a year
after they married.**

The following July, they were married. The happy couple rented an apartment in New York, and bought a home in Great Missenden near Dahl's family. They called it Gipsy House, and it was here that Dahl would create his latest hideaway: the garden shed where he worked. Dahl honeymooned in Europe with his glamorous wife, and returned to New York just as a collection of his short stories was published. Called *Someone Like You*, the book was a huge success.

The Giant Peach

Patricia Neal had been starring in a play called *The Children's Hour* when she first met Dahl. Perhaps it was a sign, because children would soon take over their lives. Their first child, Olivia, was born in 1955. Then came Tessa, in 1957, and a son, Theo, in 1960.

Dahl had used his skills as a storyteller to enter Washington society. Now he used them to step into his children's world. Each night he held them spellbound with marvellous, magical tales. Their favourite was about an orphan, James, who escapes his bullying aunts by flying to America in a giant peach full of friendly insects.

Roald and Patricia at Gipsy House with their children: Olivia, Tessa, and baby Theo.

In 1960, a second collection of Dahl's sinister adult tales, *Kiss, Kiss,* was published. His fame was growing, but Dahl was running short of ideas. So, he sent his publishers the children's story instead. *James and the Giant Peach* came out the following year. The story mixed traditional fairy-tale, black humour and comic poems, and children loved it.

James and his insect friends, in the 1997 film of Dahl's story James and the Giant Peach.

'*The peach rolled on. And behind it, Aunt Sponge and Aunt Spiker lay ironed out upon the grass as flat and thin and lifeless as a couple of paper dolls cut out of a picture book.*'
Roald Dahl, *James and the Giant Peach,* 1961.

Family Life

Roald Dahl's life, like his father's, was an extraordinary mix of soaring success and terrible misfortune. In the winter of 1960, the Dahls' nanny was pushing Theo's pram across a New York street when it was struck by a taxi. The impact shattered the four-month-old baby's skull.

Patricia Neal with her children during Theo's long recovery from his accident.

Roald Dahl with engineer friend Stanley Wade. They were a major part of the team that invented the Wade-Dahl-Till valve.

Somehow, Theo survived. But fluid built up around his brain, and a drainage tube had to be inserted into his head. A valve in this type of tube frequently became blocked, causing infection, and Theo had to have a series of dangerous operations.

Dahl always believed that when anything went wrong, he could make things better. He moved his family to Gipsy House permanently, and began working on the problem of the valve himself. Together with Stanley Wade, an engineer with whom he had once flown model aeroplanes, and Kenneth Till, a surgeon, he invented the Wade-Dahl-Till valve. By some miracle, Theo recovered without it. But the valve would be used to help thousands of injured children in the future.

'He fought misfortune as if it was a dragon to be slain.'
The *Guardian*, 1996.

The Chocolate Factory

As Theo made his recovery, a light was wired up in the writing shed so that Patricia could signal to her husband in emergencies. Dahl was always a slow, painstaking writer, and even with his ball of chocolate wrappers beside him, it was a struggle before he finished his next book.

'What distinguished Roald most of all is that he was, quite simply, a magician. Those who were lucky enough to get to know him experienced his magic powers directly. And for others, perhaps Roald became a writer so that he could cast his spells by telling them stories.'
Dahl's publisher, Tom Maschler, 'On Publishing Roald Dahl', 1997.

Dahl in his writing shed at Gipsy House, deep in thought.

A scene from the 1971 film Willy Wonka and the Chocolate Factory.

Dedicated to Theo, *Charlie and the Chocolate Factory* tells of a group of children who win golden tickets to visit Willy Wonka's chocolate factory. Here, tiny workers called Oompa-Loompas produce magical sweets. Four of the children are led by their own greed to terrible fates. But Charlie, the hero, inherits the factory. Willy Wonka is in many ways like his author. Rude and child-like, he demands that everyone play by his rules; but he is also a magician, who creates impossible wonders.

Some critics praised the humour of Dahl's latest book. Others said it was tasteless. But children loved it. By 1968, in the USA alone, *Charlie and the Chocolate Factory* had sold over half a million copies.

November

As much as Dahl's career was blessed, his personal life seemed to be under a curse. On 17 November 1962, as Theo was recovering, the Dahls' eldest daughter Olivia died suddenly after catching measles. She was seven, the same age as Roald's sister Astri when she died. Roald's grief, and the terrible echo of his father's tragedy, nearly destroyed him.

The Dahls battled on. Roald, the lover of beauty, collected hundreds of miniature plants and built a rock garden in memory of his daughter. Patricia made the film *Hud*, with Paul Newman, which would win her an Oscar. And in 1964 the Dahls had a new daughter, Ophelia.

Patricia Neal and Paul Newman, two of Hollywood's most glamorous stars, in the film **Hud.**

'Some people, when they have taken too much and have been driven beyond the point of endurance, simply crumble and give up. There are others, though they are not many, who will for some reason always be unconquerable. They have an indomitable spirit, and nothing, neither pain nor torture nor threat of death, will cause them to give up.'
Roald Dahl, *The Swan.*

But the curse continued. In 1965, Patricia, who was pregnant again and working in Hollywood, suffered three strokes. She was left crippled, blind in one eye, and unable to speak. There was another shattering blow to come. On 17 November 1967, Roald's mother, Sofie, died. It was five years, to the day, since the death of Olivia.

Wearing an eye-patch and a brace on her leg, Patricia Neal returns to England to begin her long, slow recovery.

31

The Second Miracle

The Dahl family at home after Patricia's stroke.

'As I am telling you before, I know exactly what words I am wanting to say, but somehow or other they is always getting squiff-squiddled around.'
Roald Dahl, *The BFG*, 1982.

After her strokes, Patricia had to learn to speak all over again. Her words came out muddled: a 'spoonful of sugar' became a 'soap driver'; a 'cigarette' was an 'oblogong'. Dahl would later remember this when he wrote about a tongue-twisted giant in *The BFG*.

Back at Gipsy House, Dahl organized a rota of family and friends to give Patricia hours of lessons each day. He also forced her to make speeches at public events. Some people were horrified by the way Dahl bullied his wife, but Dahl believed this was the only way she would make a full recovery. And recover she did. Their daughter, Lucy, was born in August 1965, and Patricia soon returned to acting.

The 2002 stage show of Chitty Chitty Bang Bang. *Dahl wrote the script for the film in 1967.*

Meanwhile, Dahl wrote two film scripts based on novels by his old friend Ian Fleming. One was the James Bond adventure, *You Only Live Twice*. The other was *Chitty Chitty Bang Bang*, which had some familiar characters: a hero who invents sweets, and a baddie who can smell children!

The Champion of the World

At Gipsy House, Roald Dahl had created a magical world for his children. In the garden there were a hundred different roses, brightly coloured budgies, a maze and an old gipsy caravan.

The old gipsy caravan at Dahl's home, which also appears in **Danny the Champion of the World.**

Many of Dahl's stories have been made into films, like this 1989 version of Danny the Champion of the World.

During Patricia's recovery, Roald worked tirelessly to keep this dreamworld alive. He drove his children to school still wearing his nightshirt and slippers. From the ceiling of their bedroom, he hung fifty coloured glass balls and told them the reflections would scare off witches.

Dahl's next major book, *Danny the Champion of the World*, features the type of magical father that Dahl hoped to be. Danny has no mother, but lives in a gipsy caravan with his father. He tells Danny wonderful stories; makes him kites and fire-balloons; and teaches him to drive a car at a young age – all things that Dahl did with his own children. Together, Danny and his father defeat a bullying landowner by poaching his pheasants. The story is all about Dahl's belief that a parent should not be boring, but 'sparky'.

'It was impossible to be bored in my father's company. He was too sparky a man for that. Plots and plans and new ideas came flying off him like sparks from a grindstone.'
Roald Dahl, *Danny the Champion of the World*, 1975.

35

My Father's Deep Dark Secret

As he entered his sixties, Dahl suffered increasing pain from his wartime injuries. He had a hip replacement, and placed the old bone on his writing desk.

Dahl in his sixties, enjoying fame and success.

'No father is perfect. Grown-ups are complicated creatures, full of quirks and secrets. Some have quirkier quirks and deeper secrets than others, but all of them, including one's own parents, have two or three private habits hidden up their sleeves that would probably make you gasp if you knew about them.'
Roald Dahl, *Danny the Champion of the World*, 1975.

His success continued. In 1979, Dahl's adult stories were turned into the television series *Tales of the Unexpected*, in which Dahl appeared as a sinister storyteller. Meanwhile, the artist Quentin Blake began working on Dahl's children's stories. His mischievous and funny illustrations reflect the humour shown in Dahl's writing, and were the perfect pictures for new works such as *The Enormous Crocodile*, *The Twits* and *Revolting Rhymes*.

There was also a new partnership at home. For several years, Roald had been keeping a secret. He was in love with Felicity Crossland, a friend of Patricia's. Finally, Patricia left, and Felicity moved in to Gipsy House.

This 2001 stage play captures the grotesque wildness of Dahl's story **The Twits.**

Journey to a Dream Country

Dahl used to tell his children that their dreams were created by a big, friendly giant who blew magical powders through their bedroom window. He would then say goodnight, and creep out into the garden. Easing his creaking bones up a ladder, he would slide a bamboo cane through their window, and gently blow!

The BFG *shown at the Sadler's Wells theatre in 2002, based on Roald Dahl's story.*

'*When all the other giants is galloping off every what way and which to swollop human beans, I is scuddling away to other places to blow dreams into the bedrooms of sleeping children. Nice dreams. Lovely golden dreams. Dreams that is giving the dreamers a happy time.*'
Roald Dahl, *The BFG*, 1983.

This idea led to *The BFG*, which featured one of Dahl's greatest characters. The dream-blowing BFG (Big Friendly Giant) speaks terrible English, or 'wigglish'. He drinks frobscottle, a delicious fizzy drink with sinking bubbles that cause him to 'whizzpop'. The BFG is bullied by even bigger giants until he is helped by a little orphan, whom Dahl named after Tessa's new daughter, Sophie.

At the end of the book, the BFG sneaks Sophie into the queen's bedroom at Buckingham Palace. Shortly after Dahl had finished the book, the royal bedroom really was broken into by an intruder named Michael Fagan – much to Dahl's amusement!

*Dahl named the heroine of **The BFG** after his granddaughter, Sophie, shown here with her mother Tessa.*

The Grand High Witch

Dahl had reason to be content. Gipsy House was filled with beautiful paintings and antiques that Dahl had collected. He enjoyed good food and fine wines and still handed out chocolates to his many visitors. And he was writing better than ever. He was very happy. In 1983, he married Felicity.

Dahl also enjoyed what he called his 'child power', saying if he knocked on a child's door anywhere in the world he hoped that he might be invited in for a cup of tea. On more than one occasion he arranged for orphans from Italy to visit Great Missenden and share in the magic of Gipsy House. Dahl's tales had been published everywhere from Australia to China, and in 1983 *The Witches* won him the prestigious Whitbread Prize. The judges said they were 'in the hands of a master'.

Roald and Felicity on their wedding day.

'By then I'll be a very old mouse and you'll be a very old grandmother and soon after that we'll both die together.'
Roald Dahl, *The Witches*, 1983.

Angelica Huston plays the terrifying Grand High Witch in the 1989 film of Dahl's story, The Witches.

While writing *The Witches*, Dahl clearly thought about his own life. The story recalls childhood tales from Norway, and features a witch-hunting grandmother Dahl based on his own mother. During the tale, the hero – again an orphan – is turned into a mouse. He is happy because he will live only as long as his beloved grandmother, avoiding the pain of loss that Dahl had suffered throughout his life.

The Third Miracle

Roald Dahl, aged 73, outside the hut that was his 'inventing room'.

In his final years, Dahl became a very controversial figure. He made an outspoken attack on Israel, criticized the author Salman Rushdie, and turned down an OBE because he felt he deserved a knighthood. But then he had never been afraid of offending people, which is perhaps why children love his stories.

When Dahl was diagnosed with cancer, he vowed to fight it as he had fought misfortune all his life. He continued to hobble down to his writing hut, and completed two autobiographies, *Boy* and *Going Solo*. By some miracle, he also found the energy to continue writing children's stories. *Matilda*, about a little girl who uses magical powers to defeat her bullying teacher Miss Trunchbull, became his fastest-selling book.

He also had time to collect one last thing of beauty, bidding from his hospital bed for a painting by Vincent van Gogh. On 23 November 1990, aged 74, Roald Dahl died. November was the month that had always brought him tragedy.

'She felt as though she had touched something that was not quite of this world, the highest point of the heavens, the farthest star.'
Roald Dahl, *Matilda*, 1988.

A film version of **Matilda** *was made in 1996.*

The Magic Finger

Like the inventor Willy Wonka and the dream-blowing BFG, Roald Dahl knew how to weave magic for children. That is why the characters he created in a garden shed live on today. They appear in films, plays and concerts around the world, and Dahl's books have been translated into over 30 languages. With money created by Roald's magical characters, Felicity set up the Roald Dahl Foundation to support children's health and literacy charities.

Dahl's own children have now grown up, and cherish memories of their father's bedtime stories. His granddaughter Sophie inherited both his height and his desire to write. She became famous as a supermodel, and in 2002 wrote the fairy-tale *The Man With The Dancing Eyes*.

A Dutch edition of **The BFG.** *Dahl's books have been published in many different languages.*

Dahl's granddaughter Sophie has found great fame as a supermodel.

'If you want to remember what it's like to live in a child's world, you've got to get down on your hands and knees and live like that for a week. You'll find you have to look up at all these ... giants around you who are always telling you what to do and what not to do.'
Roald Dahl, *The Roald Dahl Guide to Railway Safety.*

Some adults criticized the riotous humour of Roald Dahl's books. But he felt that they had simply forgotten what it was like to be a child. As he wrote in *The Minpins,* which was published after his death: 'Those who don't believe in magic will never find it.'

Glossary

Amputated Cut off by a surgeon.
Antiques Objects, such as furniture, that are valuable because of their age.
Appendicitis Inflammation of an organ called the appendix. These days, people rarely die from appendicitis.
Avid Enthusiastic, devoted.
Critics People whose job it is to review new books, plays and films.
Diplomat Somebody who represents their government in a foreign country.
Elevators The flaps on the tail of an aeroplane that control its height.
Enlisted Signed up to join the army, navy or air force.
Indomitable Impossible to defeat.
Majesty Dignity or beauty.

Orphans Children whose parents have died.
Pneumonia A serious infection of the lungs, which can sometimes lead to death.
Poaching Hunting or catching animals and fish on somebody else's land.
Quirks Strange types of behaviour.
Radiated Spread out from a central point.
Shipbroker Somebody who arranges supplies and passengers for ships.
Strokes Attacks caused by a change in the flow of blood to the brain, which can leave the victim with serious disability.
Valve A device that controls the flow of a fluid.
Whitbread Prize A major British prize for the writer of the year's best book.

Further Information

Books

The Roald Dahl Treasury (Jonathan Cape, 1997)

Boy and Going Solo by Roald Dahl (Puffin, 2001)

The Roald Dahl Cookbook by Roald Dahl and Felicity Dahl (Penguin Books, 1996)

Roald Dahl's Revolting Recipes by Felicity Dahl and Josie Fison (Red Fox, 2002)

Even More Revolting Recipes by Felicity Dahl and Lori-Ann Newman (Puffin Books 2003)

Roald Dahl and his Chocolate Factory by Andrew Donkin (Hippo, 2002)

Roald Dahl by Haydn Middleton (Heinemann, 1998)

As I Am by Patricia Neal (Pocket Books, 1999)

Roald Dahl: A Biography by Chris Powling (Puffin, 1994)

Roald Dahl by Jeremy Treglown (Faber and Faber, 1994)

Date Chart

1911 Harald Dahl marries Sofie Hesselberg.

1916, **13 September**, Roald Dahl is born in Llandaff, Wales.

1919 Roald's sister, Astri, dies from appendicitis.

1938 Posted to Africa by the Shell Oil Company.

1939 Joins the RAF in Kenya.

1940 Crashes his aeroplane, suffering what he calls a 'monumental bash on the head'.

1953 Marries Patricia Neal. They have five children: Olivia (1955), Tessa (1957), Theo (1960), Ophelia (1964) and Lucy (1965).

1960 Theo suffers a serious road accident, leading Dahl to invent the Wade-Dahl-Till valve.

1962 Olivia dies after catching measles.

1965 Patricia Dahl suffers three strokes. Dahl works on screenplay for *You Only Live Twice*.

1967 Roald's mother Sofie dies.

1977 Has a hip replacement.

1978 Begins working with Quentin Blake.

1979 Appears as a sinister storyteller in *Tales of the Unexpected*.

1983 Roald and Patricia are divorced. Roald marries Felicity Crossland. Wins the Whitbread Prize for *The Witches*.

1990, 23 November, Roald Dahl dies aged 74.

Works

1942: *Shot Down Over Libya*

1943: *Walt Disney: The Gremlins*

1946: *Over to You*

1948: *Sometime Never*

1953: *Someone Like You*. Adult short stories.

1960: *Kiss, Kiss*. More adult short stories.

1961: *James and the Giant Peach*

1964: *Charlie and the Chocolate Factory*

1966: *The Magic Finger*

1970: *Fantastic Mr Fox*

1972: *Charlie and the Great Glass Elevator*

1975: *Danny the Champion of the World*

1977: *The Wonderful Story of Henry Sugar*

1978: *The Enormous Crocodile*

1979: *My Uncle Oswald*. Another adult novel.

1980: *The Twits*

1981: *George's Marvellous Medicine*

1982: *The BFG; Revolting Rhymes*

1983: *The Witches; Dirty Beasts*

1984: *Boy: Tales of Childhood*. First part of his autobiography.

1985: *The Giraffe and the Pelly and Me*

1986: *Going Solo*. Part two of his autobiography.

1988: *Matilda*

1989: *Rhyme Stew*

1990: *Esio Trot*

1991: *The Vicar of Nibbleswicke; The Minpins* and *My Year* published after his death.

Index

All numbers in **bold** refer to pictures as well as text.

BFG, The 32, **38**, 39, **44**
Blake, Quentin 37
Boy 43

Cadbury's 11
Charlie and the Chocolate Factory 4, **5**, 11, **29**
Chitty Chitty Bang Bang **33**
Crossland, Felicity 37, **40**, 44

Dahl, Astri 8, 30
Dahl, Harald 6-7, **6**, 8
Dahl, Lucy 33
Dahl, Olivia **24, 26**, 30
Dahl, Ophelia 30, **32**

Dahl, Roald **4, 13, 14, 16, 21, 24, 27, 28, 31, 32, 34, 36, 40, 42**
   birth 7
   childhood 8-11
   children 24, 26-27, 30, 33, 34-35
   death 43
   diplomatic work 17
   films 19, 29, 33, 35, 41, 43
   marriages 22-23, 40
   Royal Air Force 14-16
   school 10-11, 12
   Second World War 14-19
   Shell Oil Company 12-13
   spying 18

Dahl, Sofie **6**, 7, 9, 20, 31
Dahl, Sophie **39**, 44-45, **45**
Dahl, Tessa 2**4, 26, 32, 39**
Dahl, Theo 24, 26-27, 28, 29, 32
Danny the Champion of the World 34, **35**, 36
Dar es Salaam 13
Dirty Beasts 13
Disney, Walt 19

Enormous Crocodile, The 37

films 19, 29, 33, 35, 41, 43
Fleming, Ian 18, 33
Forester, C.S. **17**

Going Solo 43
Gremlins, The 19

Hemingway, Ernest **18**
Hollywood 19, 31

James and the Giant Peach 24, **25**

Kiss, Kiss 25

Lamb to the Slaughter 20, 21

Matilda 43
Minpins, The 14, 45

Neal, Patricia 22-23, **23, 24, 26**, 28, **30, 31, 32**, 33, 35, 37
Norway 7, 9

Over to You 20

Repton School 10-11, 12
Revolting Rhymes 37
Roald Dahl Foundation 44
Roald Dahl Guide to Railway Safety, The 45
Rushdie, Salman 42

Shot Down in Libya 17
Skin 20
Someone Like You 23
Sometime Never 20
Swan, The 31

Tales of the Unexpected 37
Till, Kenneth 27
Twits, The **37**

Wade, Stanley **27**
Wade-Dahl-Till valve 27
Whitbread Prize 40
Witches, The 9, 40, **41**